Creative Director and CEO: Jason Kingsley
Chief Technical Officer: Chris Kingsley
Head of Publishing: Ben Smith
Deputy Publishing Manager: Rob Power
2000 AD Editor in Chief: Matt Smith
Senior Graphic Novel Editor: Keith Richardson
Graphic Novel Editors: Maz Smith, Oliver Pickles
Publishing Coordinator: Owen Johnson
Graphic Design: Sam Gretton, Oz Osborne & Gemma Sheldrake
Reprographics: Joseph Morgan, Emma Denton & Richard Tustian
PR: Michael Molcher

ISBN: 978-1-78108-752-7

Published by Rebellion, Riverside House,
Osney Mead, Oxford, UK. OX2 0ES
www.rebellion.co.uk

Printed in Malta by Gutenberg Press
Manufactured in the EU by Stanton Book Services Ltd., Wellingborough
NN8 3PJ, UK.
10 9 8 7 6 5 4 3 2 1

For more information on *Treasury of British Comics* graphic novels, please visit
treasuryofbritishcomics.com

ART BY

HUGO PRATT

STORY BY **DONNE AVENELL**

Battle Stations

I'm British, I have read comics my entire life. I was around for the 80s comics boom and all that followed. I have worked for *2000 AD* – the most important British comic of the last half century – for years. I have lived in Italy and am a keen admirer of the Italian maestro Hugo Pratt. I have devoured comics history and thought I knew the story of the medium in the UK.

So, with that background, finding out that Hugo Pratt illustrated a dozen book-length war stories for British publishing behemoth Fleetway and that no one had ever bothered to collect them in English was baffling. It didn't make sense and more than that it was disrespectful to the readers who would want to get their hands on these incredible tales, and it was emblematic of the disrespect with which the long history of comics in the UK had been treated.

It turned out I knew so very less about British comics history than I assumed. At the time Hugo Pratt moved to west London and worked for Fleetway in 1959, Britain's weekly comic book industry published more comics than any country on earth. Pratt had started working for Fleetway's *War Picture Library* and its sister series when he lived in Argentina, and continued in London. One of a galaxy of international greats such as Francisco Solano López and Luis Bermejo to work for the UK market via agencies, Pratt and his contemporaries would astonish and engage readers for years with work you could not find in any bookstore or library.

Fleetway and its magazine-publisher owners were never interested in the book market. After these comics had their week on the newsstands they were quietly retired to the archives, perhaps to see a reprint for a week a few years later, but before long the *Picture Libraries* were cancelled, their stories forgotten. Even when the first graphic novel boom came in the '80s and '90s the magazine companies, despite vast archives heaving with incredible stories and world class creators, could never bring themselves to publish graphic novels from their own backlist.

Clearly that situation was untenable, but if the owners didn't care about this travesty, there was little anyone else could do. Until Rebellion came along. Having first acquired *2000 AD* in the year 2000 and saved it from cancellation, we now set about acquiring the comic book rights and archives of Fleetway and its parent company IPC which had been split up and sold to different owners. It's taken years to pull together and more years to build up a team who restore artwork for the dedicated editors who, book by book, are restoring the lost history of British comics.

So finally, sixty years after these stories first appeared, Rebellion is delighted to present Hugo Pratt's extraordinary work.

To battle stations!

Ben Smith
Head of Rebellion Publishing

BATTLE STATIONS

THE WAR AT SEA IS A COLD-BLOODED WAR. ASSASSIN AND VICTIM STALK EACH OTHER ACROSS THE WINDY HORIZONS OR UNDER THE DARK WAVES, AND THEIR EYES AND THEIR HANDS ARE INSTRUMENTS. THEY KILL OR THEY ARE KILLED, BUT THEY RARELY SEE THEIR ENEMY...

... IT WAS A WRY TRICK OF FATE WHICH BROUGHT THE THREE BRITISH SEAMEN, AND THE GERMANS THEY HATED SO MURDEROUSLY, FACE TO FACE.

Chapter 1. *Mass Slaughter*

ON THE NIGHT OF JUNE 13, 1942, OFF MIAMI, THE AMERICAN TANKER, *JOHN L. HINES*, NORTHWARD BOUND, WAS HIT BY TWO TORPEDOES. THERE WAS HIGH OCTANE SPIRIT IN HER TANKS...

THE TANKER'S ESCORT WAS A BRITISH ANTI-SUB TRAWLER, THE *LOTUS*, ONE OF TWENTY-FOUR SENT ACROSS THE ATLANTIC IN MARCH TO CHECK THE SLAUGHTER. SHE HAD FAILED THIS TIME, BUT SHE STILL HAD A JOB TO DO...

WE'LL LOOK FOR SURVIVORS LATER, NUMBER ONE. LET'S GET AFTER THAT U-BOAT!

NO CONTACT ON THE ASDIC, SIR. JERRY MUST HAVE FIRED THOSE FISH FROM THE SURFACE...

THE VOICE OF LIEUTENANT RAYNER, R.N.V.R., WHEN HE SIGHTED THE U-BOAT IN THE MOONLIGHT, WAS THE UNEMOTIONAL VOICE OF A MAN GETTING ON WITH THE JOB.

THERE SHE IS, SIR! GREEN ONE-NINE. TURNING TOWARDS US!

I SEE HER, NUMBER ONE. STARBOARD FIFTEEN—GUN CREW CLOSE UP...

LEADING SEAMAN FORD, BRACING HIMSELF AGAINST THE TRUNNION OF THE QUICK-FIRER AS THE TRAWLER CAME AROUND TO STARBOARD, WAS AS MATTER-OF-FACT AS THE LIEUTENANT...

HECK! THE SKIPPER'S NOT GOING IN FOR THE KILL WITH THIS POP-GUN, IS HE?

THAT'S WHAT YOU DRAW YOUR PAY FOR, SKINNER. GET YOUR ELEVATION AND STOP BEEFING!

IT'S THEM OR US, EH! WELL, LIKE THE CHIEFY'S ALWAYS SAYING, *THERE'S A WAR ON, SKULLY!*

IT WAS THE JOB OF H.M. TRAWLER *LOTUS* TO SINK THE ENEMY, EVEN WHEN THE ENEMY WAS TWICE AS BIG AND TWICE AS POWERFUL AS HERSELF. BEARING TOWARDS THE U-BOAT AT A PLATE-SHAKING EIGHT KNOTS, THE *LOTUS* TOOK ON THAT JOB...

THE U-BOAT HAD A FOUR-INCH GUN ON THE CASING AFT OF THE CONNING TOWER. SHE FIRED TWO RANGING SHOTS AS THE *LOTUS* CLOSED. HER THIRD SHELL WAS A DIRECT HIT LOW ON THE TRAWLER'S WATERLINE.

THE SHELL STOPPED THE TRAWLER DEAD IN HER TRACKS. EVEN THEN, THERE WAS NO ANGER IN LIEUTENANT RAYNER'S VOICE...

JERRY'S TORN THE INNARDS OUT OF US, SIR. THE BOILERS HAVE GONE!

IT'S BAD LUCK, NUMBER ONE - WE DIDN'T EVEN GET A SHOT IN FIRST!

THE UPWARD-HEAVING EXPLOSION HAD BROKEN LEADING SEAMAN FORD'S ANKLE. THE PAIN WAS AGONISING, BUT HE WAS A FAIR-MINDED MAN.

ABANDON SHIP!

THE SWINE... THE SWINE!

STOW IT, SKINNER—JERRY'S ONLY DOING HIS JOB, SAME AS US!

DOWN IN THE GUTTED ENGINE-ROOM, STOKER SCULLY TOOK THE DISASTER AS CALMLY AS THE LIEUTENANT AND THE LEADING SEAMAN.

OKAY, SCULLY, THIS IS WHERE YOU HOP IT! JERRY'S DONE YOU OUT OF YOUR JOB THIS TIME.

FLAMES STILL LICKED ACROSS THE OIL-STREAKED WATER. IN THEIR HARSH GLARE, THE SURVIVORS OF BOTH SHIPS STRUGGLED TOWARDS THE RAFTS.

HELP!

HERE, MATE—GRAB!

9

A FEW YARDS OFF, LIEUTENANT RAYNER, LEADING SEAMAN FORD AND STOKER FIRST CLASS SCULLY, HAD A GRANDSTAND VIEW OF THE WHOLESALE BUTCHERY AS THE U-BOAT'S HULL CUT THROUGH THE RAFT... SPILLING ITS CARGO OF WOUNDED MEN INTO THE SEA...

THE MURDERERS! THEY DELIBERATELY RAMMED THAT RAFT!

GET DOWN, SIR! THEY'RE MANNING THE MACHINE GUN!

THERE WAS A HEAVY MACHINE GUN MOUNTED TO THE REAR OF THE U-BOAT'S CONNING TOWER. IT OPENED UP VICIOUSLY...

AAA-AGH!

THE DIRTY... UUUGH!

10

SUCH ATROCITIES WERE RARE, EVEN IN THE HARD-FOUGHT ATLANTIC BATTLE. ALL BUT THREE SURVIVORS OF THE *JOHN L. HINES* AND THE *LOTUS* DIED THAT NIGHT...

THOSE THREE MEN, LIEUTENANT RAYNER, LEADING SEAMAN FORD AND STOKER FIRST CLASS SCULLY, WERE FILLED WITH VENOMOUS HATE AT THE UNLAWFUL SLAUGHTER THEY HAD JUST WITNESSED.

11

THE U-BOAT DIVED. IT LEFT BEHIND IT A FEW SHATTERED SCRAPS OF WOOD, SOME BROKEN BODIES, AND A BITTER LEGACY OF HATRED...

AT DAWN, A HARBOUR CONTROL LAUNCH FROM MIAMI, NOSING THROUGH THE OIL SLICK AND THE UGLY WRECKAGE THIRTY MILES OFFSHORE, FOUND THE SURVIVORS...

THREE OF THEM, SKIPPER! THAT'S ALL, JUST THREE OF THEM!

HERE, JOE— YOU'RE OKAY NOW!

THE CRUISER CARRIED SIX 6-INCH GUNS AND A SECONDARY ARMAMENT OF 4-INCH AND MULTIPLE GUNS. SHE COULD HIT HARD. SHE WOULD HAVE TO HIT HARD TO SATISFY THE SURVIVORS OF THE *LOTUS* ATROCITY...

ALL RIGHT, YOU TWO — I'LL SHOW YOU YOUR ACTION STATIONS. YOU'VE JOINED THIS SHIP TO FIGHT!

JUST GIVE US THE CHANCE, CHIEF, THAT'S ALL...

THIS WAY, SIR — THE CAPTAIN WILL SEE YOU NOW.

THE YOUNG SUB-LIEUTENANT LOOKED CURIOUSLY AT RAYNER AS HE LED HIM BELOW.

THE PURSER TELLS ME YOU'RE SURVIVORS FROM A U-BOAT SINKING, LIEUTENANT.

WE SURVIVED. WE'RE GOING TO MAKE THE GERMANS WISH WE HADN'T BEFORE WE'RE FINISHED WITH THEM!

IN THE CRUISER CAPTAIN'S DAY CABIN...

SOMEWHERE IN THE SOUTH ATLANTIC, RAYNER, THE GERMAN ARMED RAIDER *MANNHEIM* IS AT LARGE. THERE'S A BATTLE SQUADRON ON HER TRACK. OUR JOB HAS TO DO WITH THAT...

BUT WE'RE NOT GOING TO GET A CRACK AT THE RAIDER OURSELVES, IS THAT IT, SIR?

AN HOUR LATER, THE *VENGEFUL* SLIPPED HER CABLES AND SET COURSE SOUTH AND EAST, WITH SIX HUNDRED MEN OF HER SHIP'S COMPANY READY TO DO THEIR DUTY, AND THREE OF THEM LUSTING FOR THE KILL...

AT LATITUDE TEN SOUTH, TWO HUNDRED MILES OFF RECIFE AND A WEEK AFTER SHE HAD LEFT NORFOLK, THE *VENGEFUL* CAME UPON HER QUARRY...

SMOKE ON THE PORT BOW, RED ONE NINE...

THE SHIPS ON THE HORIZON WERE VISIBLE NOW FROM THE BINOCULARS ON THE CRUISER'S BRIDGE. THERE WERE FOUR OF THEM, THE SUPPLY SHIP AND THREE ESCORTING DESTROYERS. THEY WERE FIVE MILES AWAY...

CALMLY, WITHOUT ANGER OR EXCITEMENT, THE CAPTAIN SET IN MOTION THE COMPLICATED WEAPON OF DESTRUCTION WHICH IS A FIVE-THOUSAND TON CRUISER OF HIS MAJESTY'S NAVY...

ACROSS THE FOUR MILES OF SEA, THE *VENGEFUL* SLUNG ITS LETHAL BROADSIDES AT AN ENEMY WHO WAS STILL ONLY A DISTANT SHAPE AGAINST THE SKYLINE...

STRADDLE, SIR. THE LEADING DESTROYER HAS STOPPED...

MASTHEAD REPORTS ENEMY CLOSING UP, SIR...

PORT TEN — REVOLUTIONS FOR THIRTY KNOTS...

THIS WAS THE WAR AT SEA, THE COLD-BLOODED WAR, DEATH AT LONG RANGE. TO LIEUTENANT RAYNER IT WAS A BITTER FRUSTRATION...

HECK, SIR! WE'RE NOT JUST GOING TO SIT OUT HERE AND PUMP SHELLS AT THE HORIZON, ARE WE? WHY DON'T WE GO RIGHT IN AND FINISH THEM OFF?

CONTROL YOURSELF RAYNER. IF WE CLOSE WE LOSE THE ADVANTAGE OF OUR MAIN ARMAMENT. ALSO WE RISK A TORPEDO ATTACK!

THE CAPTAIN'S VOICE HAD BEEN ICY. LIEUTENANT RAYNER WHEELED AWAY FROM IT ANGRILY...

GUNNERY OFFICER— CONCENTRATE ON THE DESTROYERS. I'LL KEEP THE RELATIVE BEARING CONSTANT...

ANOTHER STRADDLE, SIR. GUNS IS PICKING THEM OFF NEATLY...

BUT LIEUTENANT RAYNER COULD AT LEAST SEE THE ENEMY THROUGH HIS BINOCULARS. DOWN IN 'B' TURRET, BEHIND SIX INCHES OF STEEL PLATE, LEADING SEAMAN FORD COULD SEE NOTHING AT ALL...

HOME!

WAKE UP, FORD! GET THAT BREECH CLOSED!

ROYAL NAVY

19

FORD WAS NUMBER TWO ON THE RIGHT-HAND GUN. HIS JOB WAS TO OPEN THE BREECH AFTER EVERY SHOT AND CLOSE IT AS THE NEXT SHELL WAS RAMMED HOME. BUT HIS MIND WAS NOT ON HIS JOB...

HERE, FOR PETE'S SAKE! FORD!

TAKE OVER FROM THAT MAN, SOMEONE! JUMP TO IT!

I'VE GOT TO SEE WHAT'S GOING ON! LET ME OUT OF HERE!

TWO MONTHS OF BROODING HAD SHAKEN THE VETERAN'S SIMPLE MIND. THE OBEDIENCE OF A LIFETIME OF NAVAL DISCIPLINE HAD CRACKED IN THAT BURNING MOMENT OF FRUSTRATION...

TWO MONTHS I'VE BEEN WAITING FOR THIS... WAITING TO SEE THOSE FILTHY JERRIES SWEAT LIKE THEY MADE MY MATES SWEAT!

HE'S NOT SCARED, CHIEF— HE'S FIGHTING MAD!

ALL RIGHT, CALM HIM DOWN, KILLICK...

FOUR MILES AWAY ACROSS THE WATER, THE DESTRUCTION WHICH RAYNER, FORD AND SCULLY HAD BEEN SO EAGER TO WITNESS WAS BEING WROUGHT IN FIRE AND BLOOD...

FROM THE BRIDGE OF THE *VENGEFUL*, ALL THEY COULD SEE WERE THE THREE COLUMNS OF BLACK AND GREASY SMOKE CLIMBING AGAINST THE SKYLINE. IT WAS ENOUGH...

CEASE FIRE! STARBOARD FIFTEEN. REVOLUTIONS FOR THIRTY KNOTS. WE WILL CLOSE THE ENEMY NOW, GENTLEMEN!

TWO OF THE THREE GERMAN DESTROYERS HAD ALREADY DISAPPEARED WHEN THE *VENGEFUL* CLOSED. THE SMASHED HULK OF THE THIRD WAS SETTLING IN THE LURID WATER...

MAKE A SIGNAL TO THE SUPPLY SHIP, YEOMAN. TELL HER WE SHALL BLOW HER OUT OF THE WATER IF SHE DOES NOT HEAVE-TO IMMEDIATELY. I WANT TO PUT A PRIZE CREW ABOARD HER!

LIEUTENANT RAYNER HAD BEEN STARING WITH HUNGRY EYES AT THE WRECKAGE IN THE WATER. NOW HE TURNED EAGERLY TO THE CAPTAIN...

SIR, MAY I TAKE THE CREW ABOARD THAT GERMAN SHIP?

ALL RIGHT, RAYNER. PICK YOUR CREW FROM THE MEN WHO CAN BE SPARED. WE'LL COVER YOU WITH OUR GUNS!

THE MEN WHO COULD BE SPARED INCLUDED LEADING SEAMAN FORD AND STOKER FIRST CLASS SCULLY. LIEUTENANT RAYNER SAW THEM AMONG THE CROWD BY THE FALLS. HE PICKED THEM WITH A HARD GRIN...

ALL RIGHT, FORD — AND YOU SCULLY. WE'VE EARNED THIS!

THANK YOU, SIR!

UNDER THE WATCHFUL GUNS OF THE BRITISH CRUISER, THE THREE SURVIVORS OF THE *LOTUS* ATROCITY HEADED TOWARDS THEIR BEATEN ENEMIES...

I'M GOING TO SPIT IN THEIR FACES, THAT'S WHAT I'M GOING TO DO!

WELL, I SAY DON'T KICK A MAN WHEN HE'S DOWN!

YEAH, YOU CAN SAY THAT, SPARKS — BUT YOU HAVEN'T SEEN YOUR MATES SHOT IN THE WATER WHEN *THEY* WERE DOWN.

THE *VENGEFUL* HAD CARRIED OUT HER MISSION, BUT THE SWIFT DARKNESS OF THE SOUTHERN HEMISPHERE WAS CREEPING OVER THE SULLEN WATERS AND THE MEN ON HER BRIDGE WERE UNEASY...

HURRY THOSE BOATS UP NUMBER ONE. THESE WATERS ARE CRAWLING WITH U-BOATS. I DON'T LIKE HANGING ABOUT HERE!

AYE AYE, SIR!

THE *VENGEFUL'S* BOAT SCRAPED AGAINST THE RUSTY SIDE OF THE GERMAN SUPPLY SHIP. THERE WAS A ROPE LADDER HANGING THERE. IT WAS LEADING SEAMAN FORD WHO GRABBED IT...

SECURE, SIR...

ALL RIGHT, MEN — HAVE YOUR ARMS READY. THESE SWINE ARE FULL OF TRICKS!

THE EXPLOSION WAS DEEP INSIDE THE HULL OF THE SUPPLY SHIP. IT ERUPTED OUTWARDS WITH A SHATTERING ROAR AND A BLAST OF FLAME WHICH LIT THE WATER A MILE AWAY...

THE SUPPLY SHIP BEGAN TO SETTLE, LISTING HEAVILY. ON THE BRIDGE OF THE *VENGEFUL* MEN PEERED THROUGH THE DARKNESS HOPELESSLY AT THE LITTERED WATER...

THE JERRIES MUST HAVE PUT A TIME BOMB IN THE HOLD, SIR. THAT BOAT OF OURS WAS ALONGSIDE. I CAN'T SEE ANY SIGN OF IT...

WE CAN SPARE TEN MINUTES TO LOOK FOR SURVIVORS, NUMBER ONE. POOR DEVILS — BUT I'VE GOT TO PUT THE SAFETY OF MY SHIP FIRST.

THE BOAT HURRIEDLY LOWERED FROM THE CRUISER FOUND SIX SURVIVORS BEFORE IT TURNED BACK IN THE GATHERING DARKNESS. RAYNER, FORD AND SCULLY WERE NOT AMONG THEM...

THERE WON'T BE ANY MORE OF US, SIR. THAT SHIP BLEW UP IN OUR FACES... THE LIEUTENANT HAD JUST TOLD US TO WATCH OUT FOR JERRY TRICKS, TOO!

LET'S GO, COX'N. OUR TIME'S RUN OUT.

THE SUPPLY SHIP SANK FIVE MINUTES LATER. WHEN THE LAST FLAMES WERE ENGULFED, DARKNESS SETTLED OVER THE SEA AND THE WRECKAGE FLOATING THERE, AND THE MEN STILL SWIMMING FEEBLY THROUGH IT...

MISTER RAYNER— IS THAT YOU? I'VE FOUND A RAFT HERE!

I'M HERE, SCULLY—AND I'VE GOT FORD! HE'S EITHER UNCONSCIOUS— OR HE'S DEAD!

Chapter 2. *Face to Face*

THE HANDS SCRAPED SUDDENLY ON THE EDGE OF THE RAFT. RAYNER AND SCULLY WHEELED AT THE SOUND. THERE WERE THREE MEN CLAMBERING PAINFULLY OUT OF THE WATER...

RAYNER HAD LUNGED ACROSS THE RAFT WITHOUT THINKING. THESE MEN WERE IN THE SAME DESPERATE SITUATION AS HE WAS HIMSELF...

THE TALL MAN SMILED AT RAYNER. THERE WAS A SMALL GILT INSIGNIA ON HIS TORN SHIRT IN THE FORM OF AN EAGLE. WHEN HE SPOKE, RAYNER STUMBLED BACK, WHITE TO THE LIPS...

DANKE... DANKE! SEHR GUT...

THEY WERE ALONE ON A RAFT IN THE SOUTH ATLANTIC, THREE ENGLISHMEN AND THREE GERMANS, FACE TO FACE...

BLAZES! YOU'RE GERMANS!

JA—WE ARE GERMANS. DOES IT MATTER— NOW?

RAYNER PUT HIS HAND ON SCULLY'S ARM. THE STOKER'S BODY WAS SHAKING WITH TENSION.

LIEUTENANT RAYNER WAS TREMBLING HIMSELF. THE MEMORY OF THAT MURDEROUS NIGHT OFF MIAMI WAS SHAKING HIM WITH HATRED. BUT HE WAS AN INTELLIGENT MAN...

STOKER SCULLY WAS NOT INTELLIGENT. HE WAS A WILD ANIMAL...

31

THE TWO MEN FELL TOWARDS THE DARK WATER, THE ENGLISHMAN AND THE GERMAN, LOCKED TOGETHER IN HATRED AND DEATH...

AAAGH!

THE RAFT TILTED, ROCKED. RAYNER MOVED THEN, HARSHLY. THE TALL GERMAN TURNED SWIF'TLY BACK TO LOOK AT THE ENGLISHMAN.

SCULLY...

NO, MY FRIEND—WE CANNOT HELP THEM NOW. PERHAPS IT IS BETTER THAT WAY!

THE RAFT WAS TWENTY YARDS AWAY WHEN A HAND FEEBLY BROKE SURFACE, THEN DISAPPEARED. STOKER FIRST CLASS SCULLY HAD TAKEN HIS REVENGE...

ON THE RAFT, THE TWO MEN STARED AT EACH OTHER. THE RAGE WAS BEGINNING TO BLOT OUT THE INTELLIGENCE IN LIEUTENANT RAYNER'S MIND. HE KEPT SEEING THE BULLETS RIDDLING MEN ON ANOTHER RAFT...

SCULLY NEEDN'T HAVE DIED! IT WAS YOU GERMANS WHO STARTED IT— THE MURDER...

I DO NOT UNDERSTAND...

THERE WAS A PISTOL IN THE HOLSTER AT RAYNER'S HIP. IT MIGHT STILL WORK. HE HAD HIS HAND ON THE BUTT WHEN THE GERMAN POINTED AT FORD AGAIN...

ALL I UNDERSTAND IS THAT THIS IS A SICK MAN — AND I AM A DOCTOR. SO...

A SMALL SPARK OF HUMANITY STILL FLICKERED IN LIEUTENANT RAYNER'S TORTURED MIND. IT WAS ENOUGH TO STAY THE HAND WHICH HELD THE PISTOL...

NO—I CAN'T DO IT! NOT YET!

IT MIGHT HAVE BEEN MINUTES LATER, IT MIGHT HAVE BEEN HOURS. RAYNER HAD LOST COUNT OF TIME...

HE WILL LIVE, YOUR FRIEND, IF ANY OF US LIVE.

IT WAS IN THAT MOMENT THAT THE RAFT AND THE FOUR MEN ON IT, THE ENGLISHMEN AND THE GERMANS, WERE FLOODED SUDDENLY IN A HARSH AND GLARING LIGHT...

UGH!

THERE WAS A SHIP OUT THERE BEHIND THE SEARCHLIGHT. IT WAS CLOSING ON THE RAFT WITH QUIETLY THUDDING ENGINES. IT WAS A MERCHANTMAN...

THE TWO MEN ON THE RAFT SPOKE IN DIFFERENT LANGUAGES, BUT THE WORDS WERE THE SAME. THEY HAD BOTH STOOD FACE TO FACE WITH DEATH...

RAYNER STILL HAD NIGHTMARES. THE ANGER, THE HATRED HAD SUNK VERY DEEP. TOO DEEP, PERHAPS, FOR THE SUNLIGHT TO REACH...

NO—NOT SORRY! ONLY IT'S HARD TO BELIEVE.

BUT LOOK AROUND YOU, MY FRIEND—AT THE SUNLIGHT—AT THE FAT MEN IN THEIR DECKCHAIRS. THIS IS A WORLD AT PEACE, WHERE MEN DO NOT HATE OR FIGHT OR KILL.

THE DOCTOR WAS A DECENT MAN, RAYNER FELT THAT. BUT STILL THE ENGLISH LIEUTENANT COULD NOT FORGET THAT NIGHT OF HORROR OFF MIAMI...

AH, FRANZ. IT IS TIME FOR YOU TO CHECK ON THE INJURED ENGLISHMAN AGAIN. LET ME KNOW AT ONCE IF HE HAS RECOVERED CONSCIOUSNESS YET...

YES, POOR FORD— AND SCULLY, AND ALL THE OTHERS WHO DIED THAT NIGHT. THE MEN WHO DID IT WERE STILL GERMANS!

THE GERMAN DOCTOR HAD TENDED LEADING SEAMAN FORD FOR THREE DAYS WITH CARE AND SKILL AND GENTLENESS. FORD HAD BEEN UNCONSCIOUS ALL THAT TIME...

SO... HE DOES NOT WAKE. BUT I MUST COVER HIM UP PROPERLY OR THE HERR DOKTOR WILL BE ANGRY!

BUT IT WAS THEN, AS THE YOUNG GERMAN BENT OVER HIM, THAT THE ENGLISHMAN'S EYES FLICKERED OPEN. THE FIRST THING HE SAW WAS A SWASTIKA...

LEADING SEAMAN FORD HAD A SIMPLE MIND. THE INJURY HAD SHAKEN IT. IT REMEMBERED ONLY ONE THING, ITS HATRED FOR EVERYTHING GERMAN.

HIMMEL! HIS EYES...

THERE WAS STARK MURDER IN FORD'S EYES. THE HANDS WHICH CLAWED AT THE GERMAN'S THROAT WERE MURDEROUS HANDS. THE GERMAN YELLED IN FEAR...

THE GERMAN WAS JUST A FRIGHTENED, INNOCENT BOY. BUT IN FORD'S CRAZED MIND HE WAS THE MAN WHO HAD PULLED THE TRIGGER OF THE MACHINE GUN THAT TERRIBLE NIGHT OFF MIAMI.

RAYNER AND THE GERMAN DOCTOR WHEELED AS THE FEET THUDDED PAST THEM ALONG THE DECK. BUT THE TERRIFIED BOY HAD ALREADY REACHED THE CATWALK AND FORD WAS CLOSE BEHIND HIM...

WHAT THE DEVIL, FORD?!

DONNERWETTER!

THIRTY FEET ABOVE THE HOLD ON THE NARROW CATWALK, THE YOUNG GERMAN TURNED TO FACE LEADING SEAMAN FORD.

FORD CLOSED WITH THE BOY. THERE WAS NOTHING IN HIS FACE BUT HATRED, AND THE HUNGER FOR REVENGE...

MERCY! I HAVE DONE NOTHING TO YOU — I HAVE DONE NOTHING...

SWINE! SWINE!

YOU MURDERED MY MATES — IN COLD BLOOD!

NEIN!

STOP!

42

BUT FORD WOULD NEVER WAKE UP AGAIN. THREE BULLETS HAD HIT HIM IN THE BACK. HIS EYES WERE GLAZING AS HE JACK-KNIFED BACKWARDS OVER THE RAIL OF THE CATWALK...

ANOTHER ENGLISHMAN, ANOTHER GERMAN LAY DEAD. THE VICIOUS CIRCLE OF HATRED WAS NOT YET COMPLETED...

LIEUTENANT RAYNER HAD WATCHED IN PARALYSED HORROR WHILE FORD HAD KILLED AND BEEN KILLED. IT WAS INSTINCT WHICH MADE HIM TURN NOW, VICIOUSLY, ON THE GUARD...

YOU FOOL! GIVE ME THAT!

I-I TOLD THE ENGLISHMAN TO STAND BACK—

HE SAW THE GERMAN DOCTOR STANDING, STARING OUT TO SEA AS IF UNAFFECTED BY THE TRAGIC HAPPENINGS. A GUST OF RAGE SHOOK RAYNER...

IT MEANS NOTHING TO YOU SWINE THAT MEN DIE. THEIR LIVES ARE NOT WORTH A TUPPENNY CUSS!

LIEUTENANT RAYNER CRADLED THE GUN IN HIS ARM. HE HAD HIS FINGER ON THE TRIGGER AND HIS MIND SWAYED BETWEEN ANGER AND HORROR.

SO IT ISN'T FINISHED — THE HATRED AND THE KILLING?

Chapter 3. *Act of War*

THE SOUND WAS LIKE A LONG CLAP OF THUNDER. IT CRACKED OVER THE MERCHANTMAN OUT OF A CLEAR SKY. A HUGE COLUMN OF WATER CLIMBED OUT OF THE SEA ON THE STARBOARD QUARTER...

LIEUTENANT RAYNER WHEELED ON THE GERMAN. LESS THAN A MILE BEYOND THE GERMAN'S RIGID SHOULDER, A BULKY GREY SHADOW WAS SLIDING TOWARDS THE MERCHANTMAN.

BLAZES! THE ARMED RAIDER – THE *MANNHEIM!*

YES, MY FRIEND – I WAS WRONG! THE WAR IS NOT OVER FOR US.

THE GUN DROPPED THEN IN RAYNER'S HAND. THE SHIP'S CREW WERE CLOSE BEHIND HIM AND THE GERMAN CRIED OUT TO THEM TO LEAVE HIM ALONE...

A TIME FOR MERCY, YES...

NO — STAND BACK!

THE *MANNHEIM* HAD COME ALONGSIDE THE ARGENTINE SHIP NOW. THE SHADOWS OF HER GUNS LAY ACROSS THE SUNLIT DECK OF THE *RUY SUERTOS*...

WE HAVE SEEN NO BRITISH WARSHIPS, SENOR. BUT WE HAVE AN ENGLISHMAN AND A GERMAN ABOARD — SURVIVORS.

WE WILL SEND A BOAT FOR THEM, HERR KAPITAN. WHEN WE HAVE TAKEN THEM OFF, YOU MAY PROCEED. WE HAVE NO QUARREL WITH NEUTRALS...

FOR LIEUTENANT RAYNER, THINGS HAPPENED FAST THEN. THERE WERE MEN IN UNIFORMS ON THE NEUTRAL SHIP. THE UNIFORMS WERE GERMAN, BUT HE FELT NO ANGER.

ACHTUNG! TAKE HIM TO THE BOAT—*SCHNELL!*

YOU WILL TREAT THE ENGLISHMAN WITH RESPECT, HERR LEUTNANT. HE IS AN OFFICER — AND A DECENT MAN...

LIEUTENANT RAYNER WAS SOON SITTING IN THE STERNSHEETS OF THE ENEMY BOAT, PULLING TOWARDS THE GREAT ENEMY VESSEL OF WAR.

BUT THERE WAS NO HATRED IN LIEUTENANT RAYNER NOW. HE FACED THE GERMAN ON THE BRIDGE OF THE *MANNHEIM,* AND THERE WAS NO HATRED EVEN THEN...

YOUR NAME, LIEUTENANT? YOUR SHIP? YOU WILL ANSWER, PLEASE.

MY NAME IS RAYNER, CAPTAIN. MY SHIP IS THE *VENGEFUL.* I AM NOT OBLIGED TO GIVE YOU ANY FURTHER INFORMATION.

THIS GERMAN, THE CAPTAIN OF THE *MANNHEIM,* WAS A SEAMAN LIKE RAYNER HIMSELF. HE HAD AN ENEMY TO FIGHT AND A DUTY TO DO.

I HAVE NO FURTHER QUESTIONS TO ASK YOU, LIEUTENANT RAYNER. WE ARE BOTH NAVAL OFFICERS, NOT SPIES!

ACHTUNG! ACHTUNG!

THERE WERE THREE SHIPS HULL DOWN ON THE HORIZON. GUNFLASHES SPARKLED AGAINST THEIR DARK SHAPES. ALARM KLAXONS BELLOWED ALONG THE *MANNHEIM'S* DECKS...

BATTLE STATIONS!

THE THREE SHIPS WERE BRITISH. THE SQUADRON OF HEAVY CRUISERS HAD CAUGHT UP WITH THE GERMAN RAIDER...

TAKE THE ENGLISHMAN BELOW!

THE FIRST BRITISH SALVO HAD FALLEN SHORT. ONE SHELL OF THE SECOND SALVO SCORED A GLANCING BLOW ON THE *MANNHEIM'S* STERN AS LIEUTENANT RAYNER WAS HUSTLED BELOW...

HIMMEL!

THE CELL WAS DEEP BELOW THE RAIDER'S DECK. IT WAS A STEEL BOX WITHOUT WINDOWS. LIEUTENANT RAYNER FELT FEAR THEN, BUT STILL HE FELT NO ANGER...

I AM SORRY, HERR LEUTNANT, BUT THIS MUST BE DONE.

I UNDERSTAND, LIEUTENANT...

THE DOOR CLOSED. THE KEY TURNED IN THE LOCK. LIEUTENANT RAYNER WAS ALONE, A PRISONER, AND HIS PRISON WAS AN ENEMY WARSHIP UNDER FIRE.

THE DOCTOR— I WONDER WHAT HAPPENED TO THE DOCTOR? BUT THIS IS A HECK OF A TIME TO WONDER ABOUT THAT...

SMOKE BEGAN TO SEEP INTO THE CELL NOW. IT WAS THICK ACRID SMOKE, THE SMOKE WHICH A BURNING SHIP GIVES OFF. THE PRISONER CHOKED...

I—I'M NOT GOING TO GET OUT OF THIS— I'M GOING TO DIE DOWN HERE...

THE SHIP WAS LISTING NOW AND THE PRISONER WAS PINNED AGAINST THE WALL OF THE CELL WITH THE SMOKE BLINDING HIM...

UUGGH... UGGH!

SUDDENLY THERE WAS A COLD DRAUGHT OF CLEAN AIR IN LIEUTENANT RAYNER'S FACE AND A VOICE WAS CALLING HIM...

LIEUTENANT— LIEUTENANT! COME WITH ME!

RAYNER WAS ONLY HALF-CONSCIOUS WHEN THE MAN GRIPPED HIS SHOULDERS AND DRAGGED HIM ACROSS THE CELL. BUT HE KNEW THAT THE MAN WAS THE GERMAN, THE DOCTOR...

YOU—YOU CAME THROUGH THIS TO SAVE ME...

JA—THERE IS A TIME FOR MERCY, HEIN? BUT WE MUST BE QUICK...

LIEUTENANT RAYNER WAS A FIGHTING MAN. THERE WERE FIGHTING MEN ON THE *MANNHEIM'S* DECK, TOO. HE FELT NOW A SHARP RESPECT FOR THEM... AND PITY NOT HATE.

THUNDER! THEY'RE STILL FIGHTING!

HERR DOKTOR!

I COME...

THE DECK TILTED SHARPLY. AT THE SAME MOMENT, A SHELL BURST TEN YARDS AWAY AGAINST A SHATTERED BULKHEAD. NOW THERE WAS SOMETHING LIEUTENANT RAYNER HAD TO DO...

AAAGH!

DOC— I'M WITH YOU—

THE GERMAN WAS STILL CONSCIOUS. THE SHELLBURST HAD SAVAGED HIS LEGS YET HE WAS STILL ABLE TO GRIN THROUGH HIS PAIN AS LIEUTENANT RAYNER LIFTED HIM OFF THE DECK...

SHE'LL GO DOWN ANY MOMENT, DOC— BUT THERE'S STILL A CHANCE FOR US!

JA! THERE IS A CHANCE FOR US! SOMETIME WHEN THE FIGHTING IS OVER, FOR THE DECENT MEN, THE ENGLISHMEN AND THE GERMANS, THERE IS A CHANCE...

THE *MANNHEIM* LURCHED WEARILY. SHE WAS SINKING FAST. BUT TWO MEN, AT LEAST, JUMPED CLEAR AS SHE SLID BELOW THE WAVES.

THEY PULLED THE TWO MEN ABOARD A BOAT LOOKING FOR SURVIVORS. THE GERMAN HAD BEEN DAZED BY THE LEAP INTO THE SEA—AND IT WAS RAYNER WHO HELD HIM AFLOAT.

THE WAR AT SEA IS A *COLD-BLOODED* WAR. BUT THE HEARTS OF THE MEN WHO FIGHT IN IT ARE WARM ENOUGH.

END

War at Sea Picture Library issue 34, June 1963

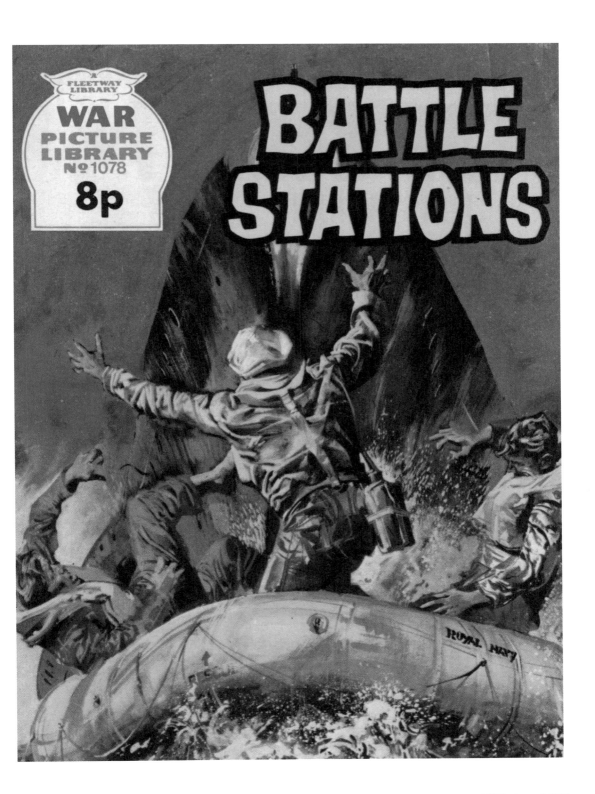

War Picture Library issue 1078, June 1975

Battle Stations was reprinted in War Picture Library 1078 (June 1975), for this reprint several of the pages had panels which were altered, these are presented on the following pages.

Alternative page 22

The lower panel on page 22 and top panel on page 23 were swapped around in WPL1078.

Alternative page 23

Alternative page 25

The lower panel of page 25 was extended to the bottom of the page to replace an advert, however the panel was redrawn by someone other than Hugo Pratt.

Alternative page 29

Scully's moustache has been altered in the 1975 version. This is most obvious on page 29.

A 3 page sequence has been transformed into a 4 page sequence by extending the quarter page panels on the first and last pages into half page panels.

Alternative page 40

Alternative page 41

Alternative page 42

Alternative page 43

Alternative page 53

These pages had their art extended to the bottom of the page to remove adverts, however unlike page 25 the art on these pages does look like Hugo Pratt, and it is possible that the advertisements were pasted over the top of his art.

Alternative page 55

TAKING TO THE SKIES!

DISCOVER MORE GREAT STORIES FROM THE

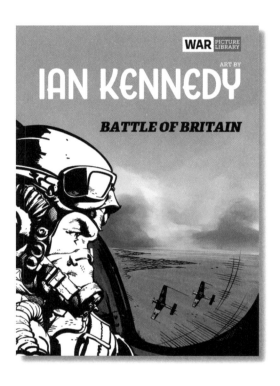

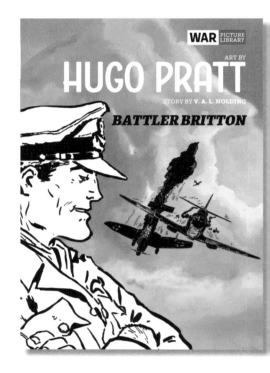

BATTLE OF BRITAIN
Art by IAN KENNEDY

Available April 2020

BATTLER BRITTON
Art by HUGO PRATT
Story by V.A.L. HOLDING

Available July 2020

HUGO PRATT

Hugo Pratt was one of the 20th century's greatest comic artists and his influence on comic art can still be felt today. Born in Rimini on July 15th 1927, his childhood was partly spent in Ethiopia where his father, a soldier in the Italian army, was stationed. It was here that he was introduced to Milton Caniff's *Terry and the Pirates*, whose style would be a huge influence on his own. After his father's capture by British troops and subsequent death from disease as a prisoner of war Pratt returned to Italy in 1943 and became an interpreter for the Allied army for the rest of the war. He began drawing comics in 1945, but it was when he moved to Argentina in 1949 that he started to find his artistic voice, meeting fellow artists Alberto Breccia, Francisco Solano López and Héctor Germán Oesterheld, with whom he created *Sgt. Kirk* and *Ernie Pike*.

In 1959 he moved to London where he worked for Fleetway drawing sixty-four page war stories that appeared in **Battle Picture Library**, **War Picture Library**, **War at Sea Picture Library** and **Battler Britton**. In 1967 he created the internationally popular comic book character Corto Maltese, for the **Sgt. Kirk** magazine, and two years later new Corto stories were created for the French magazine **Pif Gadget**. In the eighties he wrote scripts for Milo Manara, and together they created such graphic novels as *El Gaucho* and *Indian Summer*. He won countless awards for his work and was made a Knight of Arts and Letters by the French Minister of Culture before he died in 1995.

DONNE AVENELL

Donne Avenell's career in comics started before the outbreak of World War II when he was an assistant editor with Amalgamated Press working on **Radio Fun**. After serving in the navy, he returned to the company, now as an editor on an architecture magazine, while also writing radio dramas and romance stories.

In the 1950's Avenell was a prolific writer on **War Picture Library** and then **Lion**, penning such classic strips as *The Spider, The Phantom Viking, Adam Eterno* and *Dr. Mesmer's Revenge*. By the 1970's he was working on a number of projects including co-writing *Powerman* (the Nigerian superhero comic illustrated by Dave Gibbons and Brian Bolland) and **The Sun** newspaper strip *Axa*. In the same decade, Avenell also found work in the television industry, where he wrote scripts for popular spy programme *The Saint*. Later he would work with artist John Burns on both an official comic book adaption of Prince Charles and Lady Diana's wedding, and a newspaper strip called *Eartha* which ran in the **News of the World**.